GETTING REV[IEWS] FOR AMAZON FBA

A Beginners' Guide to Getting Amazon FBA Reviews to Build a Profitable Amazon Business of Private Label Products and Generate Passive Income

BOOK DESCRIPTION

Amazon has introduced new review policies focused on enhancing honesty and integrity. Many sellers have had their accounts inadvertently banned as a result of either not being aware of these policy changes or making inadvertent mistakes resulting into violation of these policies.

It is no doubt that Amazon FBA is the most popular option for many sellers on Amazon. Yet, it relies heavily on reviews to attract potential customers, push up sales and make profits. This book has been written specifically to help Amazon FBA sellers to achieve this in the most legit way without violating Amazon Review policy.

This book is intended for both FBA veterans, new and potential FBA entrants. Thus, it starts from the basic approach by introducing what Amazon FBA is and what it actually entails. If you are already using Amazon FBA, it is good to refresh your knowledge and gain new insights and perspectives. If you have never traded on Amazon, this is a great introduction to Amazon FBA.

Building up on the basics, this book dwells further into the world of reviews. It not only provides information on the mechanics of a review in ecommerce but goes deeper into its heart and soul. This way, you are able to better understand why reviews are important to Amazon FBA.

Once you gain an understanding as to why reviews are important to Amazon FBA, you can really begin to appreciate the latest changes to the Amazon Review System. You will begin to see why these changes serve your greater good rather than being a punitive and unnecessary disruption to your business as some sellers seems to feel.

Mistakes do occur. Yet, they do have consequences. You cannot avoid their costs. Review mistakes that violate Amazon Review policy are extremely costly and could permanently injure your Amazon FBA business. You can't dare miss your storefront on this world's largest online marketplace. It would be insane. Thus, it is imperative for you to know mistakes to avoid while getting reviews so as to avoid being banned. This book informs you about these mistakes and how to avoid them.

Mastering legal ways to get Amazon FBA reviews is like establishing your own goldmine on Amazon. You are guaranteed long-term value for your high quality products. In this book, you are provided with proven, practical hands-on legal ways to make genuine Amazon FBA reviews that not only helps you to avoid being banned but also enables you to leverage your reviews to push-up sales and earn supernormal profits.

Enjoy reading!

GIFT INCLUDED

If you are an entrepreneur, an aspiring entrepreneur, someone who is trying to create additional income stream, or even someone who just loves self improvement books; then you need to read my recommendations for top 10 business books ever. These are book that I have read that have changed my life for the better.

ABOUT THE AUTHOR

George Pain is an entrepreneur, author and business consultant. He specializes in setting up online businesses from scratch, investment income strategies and global mobility solutions. He has built several businesses from the ground up, and is excited to share his knowledge with readers.

DISCLAIMER

CONTENTS

INTRODUCTION

Reviews, if legit, are the best form of endorsement you could ever get on Amazon. Yet, many sellers struggle to get legit reviews for their great products simply because they lack sufficient knowledge, information and skills on how to make legit reviews.

Gone are the days when unscrupulous and dishonest sellers would fraudulently acquire fake reviews. Changes in Amazon FBA Review policy have thrust a fatal blow to their devious schemes. Unfortunately, there are many crooks out there who still ensnare desperate and gullible sellers into making fake reviews.

To save you from becoming a victim of review scams, this book provides with updates on latest changes to the Amazon FBA review system so that you are aware of them and your responsibility. It also reminds you of mistakes to avoid while making/getting reviews so that you don't get banned due to avoidable mistakes.

Having honest, legit reviews not only improves your profile but also boosts your confidence to do more, builds your goodwill and lets you attract premium price for your products so you can earn supernormal profits.

This book is the best guide for you on how to make legit reviews to avoid being banned by Amazon, leverage your reviews to push-up sales and earn supernormal profits.

Keep reading!

WHAT IS AMAZON FBA?

Amazon FBA is a system devised by Amazon to enable sellers to deliver products to Amazon's marketplace without directly incurring the normal transaction process that goes on between the buyer and the seller. In this case, Amazon acts as intermediary between the seller and the buyer.

FBA is an acronym for 'Fulfillment by Amazon'. Fulfillment is a special term in trade which refers to the process of honoring the terms of order from a customer by the vendor. In essence, the order is fulfilled when it is honored.

The fulfillment process

Fulfillment process involves all those stages in which goods move from the vendor's point to the buyer's point within a marketplace. These include;

- Warehousing – Amazon receiving and keeping products in safe and good condition on behalf of the vendor at Amazon stores while awaiting customer Orders.
- Order processing – Amazon acting on Order presented by customer on behalf of the vendor.

- Billing – Amazon requesting for payment from the Customer on behalf of the vendor after delivering as per the customer's Order.
- Returns and exchanges – Amazon honoring customer's demand for delivery to conform to the Order.
- Payment processing – Amazon processing payment on behalf of and to the vendor.
- Customer service support – Amazon rendering customer support services on behalf of the vendor.

How fulfillment by Amazon works

Fulfillment by Amazon is simply letting Amazon carry out your fulfillment functions on your behalf. In this regard, you actually outsource your fulfillment function to Amazon.

As a vendor, you deliver your products to Amazon's designated stores for purposes of fulfillment. The following are steps taken in the fulfillment process;

Step 1: Deliver your product to Amazon

Amazon has designated stores for purposes of fulfillment. Select the store near your marketplace.

Step 2: Amazon stores your products in its inventory

Once you deliver your product to a fulfillment center, Amazon takes charge of managing your inventory.

Step 3: Customers buy your product

A customer visits Amazon marketplace (via the Amazon product page) and places an order for your product.

Step 4: Amazon picks and packs the product on your behalf

Once the customer does the checkout, Amazon prepares the product into the right package as per the quantity ordered.

Step 5: Amazon delivers the product to your customer

After packaging, Amazon delivers the product to your customer as per the terms of delivery. In case of Amazon Prime members, this is a door-to-door delivery. For non-prime members, Amazon delivers to the nearest drop zone. Parcel delivery services can also be used depending on the customer specifications.

Step 6: Amazon bills the customer and receives payment on your behalf

Upon successful delivery, Amazon bills the customer and receives payment on your behalf. However, in most cases, this is done based on Cash-With-Order (Checkout) terms. Nonetheless, it is only upon successful delivery that the bill becomes due and payments become valid.

Step 7: Amazon channels payment to your bank account

On completion of successful billing process, Amazon channels payment received from customer to your bank account. This payment is net-off charges. Thus, Amazon deducts its own charges and remits the balance. Also, there is a security period. The security period allows provision for returns from customers. If the customer does not return goods within the warrant period, then, the customer is deemed to have been satisfied with the product or as having forfeited the right to return. An extra period is provided for by Amazon, in addition to the warrant period just to cater for likely delays in the return process.

What is the rationale of outsourcing fulfillment to Amazon?

Why outsource fulfillment? Like any other service that one outsources, the following are basic guiding criteria for outsourcing fulfillment service;

- When it becomes more expensive to render the service in-house
- When it becomes more productive to focus on the core functions and thus the need to outsource non-core functions

- When the level of expertise required to render the service is such complex that it cannot be economically met in-house
- When the scale of operation is too big to be met in-house e.g. international delivery networks that requires extensive logistics infrastructure
- When it is more economical, effective and efficient to do so

How do you become an FBA vendor?

First and foremost, you must meet eligibility criteria in order to become FBA vendor. After ascertaining that you have met this criteria, follow the next steps;

1. Get all relevant information required to open Amazon Seller Account
2. Open Amazon Seller Account
3. Setup your Amazon Seller profile

Information you need to know before registering for Amazon Seller Account

- Profile

- Business information to provide

- Amazon policies

- Selling plans

- Reviews policy

How to create a Great Profile

A profile is the way you present your storefront to convey a certain deliberate message about your enterprise. However, for purposes of uniformity of details in Amazon marketplace, the following are key details that you need to provide for your profile;

Business logo – A logo helps to reinforce memory about your business in the visitor's perspective. Thus, the logo should be attractive, appealing and less detailed so that it is easy for a visitor to memorize. Amazon profile has a logo section where you can upload and insert your logo image.

About – It is important to describe what your business is about in a brief, clear, concise, succulent and informative manner. There is a text area provided for you to type or paste these details about your business/product on your Amazon profile.

Shipping Information – Shipping Information is crucial to customers since Amazon is a global marketplace. Customers would definitely like to know terms of delivery well in advance before they make a buy decision. Amazon provides a section on your profile where you insert this information including your shipping terms, shipping duration, among others.

Return and refund – Customers are always concerned about seller's return policy. They would like to know whether they have a right to return faulty items and whether they will be refunded or not. They also would like to know the conditions; are they allowed to make returns? Under what terms can they claim refund? Also of critical importance, buyers would like to know before buying your product as to whether it has a warranty or not, and the duration of such a warranty, if it does exist. Amazon recognizes this and provides a Return and Refund section for you to specify return and refund policy and terms.

Privacy policy – There are certain products and services that require privacy in terms of disclosures. Examples of such products include sex therapy products, sex pleasure gadgets etc. Thus, the seller is likely going to create a privacy policy to protect both parties against undue exposure. In the same breath, consumers of such products would want to be assured that their information won't be publicized by the seller for purposes of advertisement. Hence, privacy policy becomes a necessity. Amazon too has provided space for you to insert your privacy policy, where necessary.

Business information you need to provide

It is important to provide information about your business so that customers and visitors are able know your status and other relevant details regarding it. The following are important details that you need to provide;

- Legal business name
- Bank routing and account numbers
- Brand name
- Physical location from which item will be shipped (for FBA, Amazon takes full charge)
- Customer service contact – phone and email address

Amazon policies likely to affect your business

It is very important to know and understand various Amazon policies affecting your business. A lot of people overlook policies. Yet, as often said 'the devil is in the details'. Yes, it is because of a lack of knowledge of the details that you will find yourself unknowingly or negligently flouting Amazon policies. This may result in penalties, surcharges, suspensions and even a bann. The following are important Amazon policies that you need to read, understand and keep in mind;

- <u>Product detail page rules</u>
- <u>General policies and agreements</u>
- <u>Prohibited seller activities and actions</u>
- <u>Shipping policies</u>
- <u>Selling policies</u>

Selling plan options

The following are two types of selling plans offered by Amazon;

1. **Individual**
2. **Professional**

Advantages of individual plan

1. **Low startup cost** - You only pay for what you sell (at $0.99 per item). This is a great option for startups as they are not overloaded by overhead costs.
2. **Lower risk of losses** - As you are not charged $39.99 (for professional plan), you don't risk any money. You sell zero, you are charged zero!

Disadvantages of individual plan

1. **Limited markets** - Unlike the professional plan where you can sell in a combination of several markets (e.g. US, UK and Canada), the individual plan only allows you to sell in one market (e.g. US or UK or Canada only)

2. **Less optimization facilities** - You cannot enjoy benefits of Amazon Marketplace Web Service (bulk listing and reporting tools)
3. **Less customizations** - You cannot customize your shipping rates
4. **Fewer customer incentives** - You cannot offer special promotion and gift wrap options (except for software, entertainment medium (Videos, DVDs and Music and books)
5. **Less exposure** - You are not eligible for top placement on product details page

Advantages of professional plan

1. **Unlimited variety** - Unlimited amount of products
2. **Low variable cost** - No fee per item (which is extremely expensive with large volumes)
3. **Multiple income streams** - Opportunity for more income streams
4. **Extra facilities** - Enjoy benefits of Amazon Web Service (bulk listing and reporting tools)
5. **Customer incentives** - Offer special promotion and gift wrap options (which increases your sales, boosts customer

satisfaction and increases your chances of positive reviews)

6. **More exposure to customers** - You are eligible for top placement on product details page (which boosts your brand recognition and likely to increase sales)

Disadvantages of professional plan (for small scale beginners)

- The only disadvantage of the professional plan if you are a beginner is the fixed cost of $39.99 per month. You pay this amount regardless of the number of sales you achieve.

Which seller plan is ideal for you?

If you anticipate selling less than 40 items per month, go for individual plan. However, if you anticipate selling more than 40 items per month, go for professional plan. If you are a starter, it is prudent to start with individual plan and then scale up to professional plan when you are certain that your sales per month are consistently above 40 items and likely to grow.

How to open your Amazon Seller Account

Steps:

1. Visit the registration site – <u>Amazon Seller Central</u>
2. Create a new account or use your already existing one
3. Set up your seller profile

4. Activate Feedback option and policy

How to setup your Amazon Seller Profile

To make it easy for you to create your profile, Amazon has provided step-by-step forms to enable you to set up your seller profile. Key areas of your seller profile that Amazon will help you setup are;

- Account information
- Login settings
- User permissions
- Fulfillment option (either FBA or FBM)
- Return settings
- Shipping settings
- Tax settings
- Your info and policy
- Gift options
- Notification preferences

WHY REVIEWS ARE IMPORTANT ON AMAZON FBA

The customer is always king. Suppliers are his/her employees. Like in any such arrangement, the king has to review performance of his employees. This review can mean a promotion, demotion or even firing of an employees. In as much as many vendors never see this reality as it is never so direct, the death of many enterprises and losses of some others from their coveted positions means that the king takes action, however indirect and slow its effects could be.

It is the duty of every employee to win deserved recognition from his boss/king. This is the most important non-monetary reward that a dedicated employee can get. Yet, as we surely know, some servants employees choose to enslave themselves to gain this recognition. On the other hand, some use trickery, flattery, and some other devious unconventional means to achieve this recognition. However, that which is fraudulent, regardless of its 'successes', never lasts. If discovered, the negative reputation would not only erase the fraudulently achieved positive reputation but also leave a huge negative dent.

As we shall see later, the king doesn't like being cheated and will always frown at such endeavors. Amazon, being where kings come to be served, is always taking kings' complains with seriousness deserved. Thus, there are changes that keep coming about in an endeavor to reflect the express will of the kings. We shall see this in the next two sections.

It benefits you not, in any way, to engage in slaving yourself or using trickery and fraudulent means to win the Kings' recognition. There are legal ways by which you can get deserved and assured positive recognition. We shall find out in our last section in this book.

From the foregoing, it is clear that winning the kings' recognition is extremely important. Indeed, it is the only way an enterprise can survive in the marketplace. Amazon marketplace is no exception. Amazon marketplace, being a global marketplace, has to do its best to reflect the will of the kings by keeping the best international standards. Otherwise, Amazon too will have to be punished by Kings when they stop visiting its marketplace. Kings are at their discretion to express their pleasure and displeasure at any given service. This is expressed through their reviews. It is your duty to ensure that you don't deliberately and willfully cause displeasure so that they can grant you a positive review.

To be able to understand how reviews come about (not just about who writes them and how they are written), we need to gain an in-depth understanding of the marketplace and its underlying principles. Yes, we have to dig up to the spirit of the review and its soul before being able to really appreciate the nature of its physical body (the words).

The principles of a marketplace

To be able to find why reviews are such important, it is good to understand the mechanics of a marketplace that cause the need for these reviews.

The marketplace is a place where buyers and sellers meet in order to exchange products (goods and/or services). In marketing, a product represents not just the physical good, but also all efforts carried out to create and enhance utility of that good. Thus, a product must inevitably have commensurate service. It is a mix of both goods and services. It contains the three most basic types of utility;

1. **Place** – This place refers to the marketplace. Without the product being delivered to the market, it has no utility to the buyer.
2. **Form** – This refers to the nature in which the product is delivered. This includes both its intrinsic and extrinsic features. The intrinsic features include its ingredients, how

the ingredients are combined, the texture, native color, frshness/newness, etc. Extrinsic features include shape, color enhancements, packaging material, blending, etc.

3. **Time** – The product must be delivered at such a time that best-meets buyer's consumption needs. This is crucial to customer satisfaction.

A marketplace is the central place of every capitalistic system. It is the needs of the markets that drive production.

In every capitalistic system;

1. There is always competition between buyers and between sellers.
2. There is always sacrifice and reward (positive or negative) for effort.
3. There is democracy in terms of freedom of choice.

Competition between buyers

Buyers compete for your service. The greater your product is, the stiffer the competition between buyers to get it. On the other hand, the poorer your product is, the lower is the competition between buyers to get it.

In this competition, the marketplace turns into some form of an auction yard. Like any auction, this competition is reflected in how much buyers are willing to sacrifice to acquire your product. As the buyers compete, each buyer tries to place a higher bid to outdo the others.

Those buyers who win in this competition feel happy. They become satisfied kings who are willing to promote you, at least, in non-monetary terms. This promotion comes in their report about their experience with your product. This report is what we call review.

Competition between sellers

In a capitalistic marketplace such as Amazon, sellers compete among themselves to receive vantage attention and commensurate reward from their kings. Kings largely trust each other than they do trust unknown sellers. Thus, a seller with a vote of endorsement (positive review) is likely going to receive competitive advantage in terms of attention as compared to other servants. It is just like when an employee seeks a job. Other factors being the same, the one with the best references will more likely get the job. Yes, a seller with the best references (in this case, reviews) gets the job to serve the king!

This is how sellers compete among themselves to get an opportunity to serve their king. At what reward? It is quite evident, just as in the labor market, an employee with good references (which is a clear testimony of experience) is more likely to negotiate for higher salary than a one with less or poor references. This indeed happens on the Amazon marketplace. Those sellers with great reviews can actually set a higher price for their products, yet sell more compared to those with poor or no reviews.

If sellers have the same attributes, in terms of quality of service and references, then, due to competition, they are more likely to harm each other by cutting down their price so as to attract the king's attention. This is, in essence, a form of slaving for rewards. Because, when they cut each other, their profit bleeds. This is a loss. If the loss exceeds the cost of their existence, they die out of the market. Thus, it is evidently clear that, to avoid this cut-throat competition, you have to offer an excellent product/service that saves you from the cut-throat competition. This excellent product/service, will grant you positive reviews and you will gain greater rewards.

Sacrifice and reward

In economics, every effort portends sacrifice and is geared towards a certain reward.

In a marketplace, this sacrifice is the cost and its reward is the price. The positive difference between the price and the cost is the net gain for the entrepreneurial effort. This net gain is called profit (positive reward). On the other hand, there can also be a negative difference between price and cost. This becomes a net loss. Net loss is a punishment (negative reward) from the kings for poor entrepreneurial effort to serve them.

Review in itself is a reward. The sacrifice to earn this reward is represented in the quality assurance, great service, warrants and guarantees.

Democracy as expressed in the freedom of choice

In an international marketplace such as Amazon marketplace, there are so many buyers and sellers such that no single buyer or seller can single-handedly influence the price. It is just like a large democratic nation such as United States,- there is no way one voter alone, on his/her own, can single-handedly vote to determine who the next president becomes.

While in politics the ballot is used as a vote, in the marketplace, the dollar is used as a vote.

Every dollar received from a customer is in itself not only a reward but vote of confidence to your entrepreneurial endeavor. It is a vote for the continuity of your enterprise. Like a politician, you have to endeavor to make your product more appealing to customers' satisfaction so as to receive more votes.

Just as politicians need endorsements to win over those potential but doubtful voters, you too need endorsements in form of reviews from your previous and existing customers to win over customer confidence.

You could choose to 'buy' these endorsements. But, for so long as they are not genuine, they will still reflect their absence of authenticity to the discerning eyes. You need to work for genuine endorsements. You have to offer a great product that pleases the kings. You have to serve them well.

Deceiving voters doesn't guarantee you leading them. They could protest against you (negative reviews), seek to suspend you (return goods and demand refund), or otherwise, fire you (get you banned). Kings always prevail. Customer is king.

Why are reviews such important on Amazon FBA

We have used the very important analogy that CUSTOMER IS KING. In this analogy, we have discovered that the SELLER Is an employee. We have also established that, like great employment references get one to have higher chances of winning a better-paying job, so do great reviews.

One critical term that we must not overlook is FULFILLMENT. This term has both intrinsic and extrinsic meaning. The intrinsic meaning is SATISFACTION and the extrinsic meaning is TRANSACTION (in terms of the processes and activities undertaken in transacting the Order on the seller's part to its final delivery). It is in the intrinsic meaning that the essence and power of reviews become apparent. Thus, TRANSACTION + SATISFACTION = POSITIVE REVIEWS

Thus, we can easily establish the following as the important benefits of reviews;

- Reviews enable the buyers to have confidence in the seller's products – genuine reviews are 'votes of approval' of the product's fitness for purpose. This is an endorsement of the product to potential buyers. This helps to simplify their buy decision since, subconsciously the will asking themselves "if this product served them well, why not me?"
- Reviews enable sellers to attract more customers – Most customers on Amazon marketplace have a tendency of gauging a products by its number of quality positive reviews. Thus, a product with a higher number of quality positive reviews will attract more customers than that

without. And one with high number of negative reviews will repel customers.

- Reviews enable the seller to fetch higher price for his/her product – When you have a high volume of quality positive reviews, buyers fiercely compete among themselves to buy your product. This is a cue that you can raise your price. This way you get a premium price for your product which enables you to earn supernormal profits.

- Reviews shield the seller from cut-throat competition – sellers compete in the market for buyers, especially if the products are homogenous in nature. In this case, to create an impression of uniqueness in the mind of the potential buyers, you have to do product differentiation. Product differentiation simply refers to tweaking product features so as to make one homogenous product distinguishable from others. You can differentiate your product by unique branding, altering its content, and or increasing your quality service. This way, customers will be more satisfied and feel that it deserves more endorsement than other homogenous products in the market. You are likely going to get more reviews than the rest. These reviews will raise you above the crowd thus shielding you from the stiff cut-throat competition.

- Reviews represents the Goodwill owned by the seller which are rewarded by increased patronage by customers thus resulting in higher rewards (profits) to the seller – Goodwill represents that unique value that you get which is beyond the ordinary conduct of trade. When you have above-average number of high quality reviews, all reviews that are above-average represents your Goodwill. Goodwill is an asset (donated to you freely by your by your king). Like your other assets, Goodwill helps you to generate more revenue. Yes, GOODWILL = POSITIVE REVIEWS

- Reviews increase the value of the seller's activity thus enabling the seller not to enslave oneself in order to earn – We have seen how reviews help you to fetch a premium price. This helps you earn the same or higher revenue for fewer items. When you sell fewer items, the cost of turnover goes down. Fewer items mean a lower level of activity and much less sweat. Less sweat means less effort to earn. Of course, as a shrewd business person, you would want to sell more provided that there is a market. Thus, you may not necessarily sell fewer items as a whole but fewer items per every unit of profit generated.

The relationship between Reviews, Goodwill, Premium Price and Supernormal Profit

Goodwill (positive reviews) enables you to earn a premium by charging premium price. PREMIUM = PREMIUM PRICE –

NORMAL PRICE. It is by charging premium price that you can derive supernormal profits (profit above normal profit). Premium price and supernormal profits are only enjoyed by those servants closest to the heart of the master. Yes, those who rise above the crowd by rendering exceptional, exemplary and excellent service.

THE LATEST CHANGES TO THE AMAZON FBA REVIEW SYSTEM (THE ONE THAT BANS INCENTIVIZED REVIEWS)

The only thing that doesn't change is change itself. Change is growth. Change is improvement. Change is development. Amazon would not achieve such an enviable global position if it didn't embrace change.

Amazon has created new changes of late which are clearly reflected in Amazon review policy.

What are these changes?

1. **Strict verification of customers** – Amazon endeavors to verify customers in terms of ensuring that only genuine customers are allowed to make reviews. This way, those vendors who illegally and fraudulently incentivize non-genuine customers to make reviews about their products are weeded out. This ensures that potential buyers are not mislead into buying products they would have not otherwise bought had the review information not been misrepresented.

2. **Amazon Vine program** - Amazon will invite reviewers through its vine program to make reviews. The only avenue left for incentivized reviews is through Amazon vine. However, as we shall see later, reviewers are specifically invited and vetted and only allowed to make independent and unbiased review based on their very own experience in consuming sample products selected and availed to them by Amazon.

3. **No seller invitation for reviews** - You cannot invite potential customers to make reviews on your product's profile – Amazon strictly insist only customers who have bought, used and experienced a particular product are allowed to make reviews.

4. **No discounts for reviews** - You can offer discounts and coupons but they must not be geared towards inviting beneficiaries to make reviews on your product's page. Prior to latest policy, it was common for sellers to invite customers to make reviews on their Amazon's product page. This has been disallowed. You can no longer invite customers to make reviews. Customers should make reviews out of their very own volition without coercion, duress or undue influence.

5. **No negative reviews against your competitor** - You cannot make reviews on your competitor's products with a desire to hurt your competitor's reputation. You cannot be an independent and unbiased reviewer when dealing with a competitor's products. Thus, you are discouraged from knowingly and deliberately making a review of your competitor's products.

What is the aim of these changes?

1. **Enable potential buyer make informed decision** – Amazon aims to boost customer experience. A customer who has been mislead into buying a product that he/she would have otherwise not bought without misrepresentation of facts is not the kind of customer who will have great experience. Thus, to allow customers to have a great experience, they must be encouraged to make their own independent, yet informed decision. Thus, a review should be targeted at providing factual information from an independent third-party perspective rather than a biased seller's agent who is being induced to make a positive review.

2. **Create a level playing field among sellers** – Sellers compete among each other to net in a customer. Thus, without policies aimed at controlling their behaviors, they are more likely to engage in devious schemes to outdo

each other. Some sellers have been known to hire reviewers to make negative reviews of their competitors' products or make misleading claims about their products. To ensure a level playing field among sellers, Amazon discourages incentivizing reviews in whatsoever manner, except via Amazon Vine. It also discourages sellers to review their competitors' products.

3. **Protect reputation of Amazon marketplace** – Amazon has been facing the challenge of a huge volume of incentivized reviews. Most incentivized reviews are exaggerated. Thus, they mislead buyers into erroneously making a buy decision. This makes buyers doubt Amazon marketplace and feel Amazon is somehow conspiring in this or is responsible for it. Thus, Amazon is protecting its own reputation by insisting on legit reviews.

4. **Enable customer to have better buyer experience** – Amazon is trying to ensure good information is provided in genuine reviews. Customers understand what to expect and thus won't feel cheated and thus have negative experiences.

What is forbidden?

In these changes to the review system the following are forbidden;

- **Nagging customers for reviews** – Nagging customers to make favorable reviews is not only unethical, fraudulent but also lowers customers' experience.

- **Misrepresenting facts** – Misrepresenting facts about a product, for example; exaggerating its quantity, quality, efficacy and duration lowers customer's experience. It also lowers Amazon marketplace reputation.

- **Deceiving buyers** – Deceiving buyers by making offers which you are not going to fulfill is a fraud. It not only lowers customers' experiences but also Amazon marketplace reputation. Yes, some customers have been conned into making positive reviews in order to earn certain gifts; only for those who conned them to disappear without fulfilling their promise.

- **Making reviews based on monetary inducements** – Inducements of any sort, aimed at incentivizing customers to make reviews are a form of corruption. It lowers both the buyer's and seller's dignity while denying potential buyers the right to make informed buy decision.

What is encouraged?

Amazon is endeavoring to encourage the following;

- **Unbiased reviews** – These are reviews that are not aimed at favoring the seller. Thus, the person making the review must not be one who is biased, easily compromised or lacks decision-making autonomy.
- **Genuine reviews** – These are reviews that are honestly made from unbiased customers from their very own experience of consuming the product under review.
- **Genuine efforts** – Sellers must earn reviews from their very own genuine effort to ensure that customers have great experience of their products.
- **Better quality products** – Great reviews are for better quality products. Thus, by insisting on genuine, honest and unbiased reviews, Amazon seeks to exert pressure on sellers to boost quality of their products for a greater customer experience.
- **Improved customer experience** – Amazon always endeavors to ensure the best customer experience from products available on its marketplace. Thus, those sellers who have improved customer experience not only receive great reviews from customers but also receive rewards

from Amazon by extending to them facilities that are not ordinarily available to regular sellers. Such facilities include Buy box, Amazon Vine Program, Seller Fulfilled Prime, Best Seller, etc.

MISTAKES TO AVOID WHILE GETTING REVIEWS – THESE WILL GET YOU BANNED

To be human is to err. The difference between error and mistake is that mistakes are due to negligence while errors are due to unavoidable circumstances.

Well, we all make mistakes. However, we must face responsibility for our mistakes. Responsibilities cannot exist without costs. The ultimate cost of making Amazon review mistake is being banned.

You don't have to risk being banned from trading on Amazon – the world's largest online marketplace. This is a huge loss that could mean shut-down for many businesses trading on Amazon.

Luckily, Amazon has provided elaborate information regarding its review policy such that you don't need to make mistakes. In this section, we are going to dwell into some of these mistakes discussing some of the risks that can cause them, what they are and how to avoid them.

What could make it easy for you to make review mistakes?

Mistakes are, more often than not, triggered by certain attitudes necessitated by the prevailing mindset. Most bad attitudes are due to ignorance. As such, it is important to understand the cause of those attitudes and deal with them so as to have the right attitude. With the right attitude, chances of mistakes are minimized.

The following are some of the factors that could lead to wrong attitude in as far as Amazon FBA Review policy is concerned;

1. Not understanding Amazon FBA Review policy intents
2. Not appreciating the long-term benefits of the review policy
3. Not appreciating the cause of change in the policy

The mistakes to avoid

1. Don't subscribe your account to programs that offer potential customers incentives to make reviews
2. Don't create fake customers by paying them to buy products so that they can leave reviews
3. Don't be the one writing reviews that will bestow you direct financial benefits
4. Don't offer monetary inducements in exchange for a review

5. Don't accept a unverified review – that is, reviews not triggered by buyer's actual experience of the product
6. Don't offer promotional codes or discounts in exchange for reviews
7. Don't engage in blackmailing your competitor by giving negative reviews designed to lower his/her reputation
8. Don't engage non-independent persons (e.g. friends, relatives, colleagues, spouses, fiancés, etc) to make reviews
9. Don't offer someone else positive reviews in exchange for his/her positive reviews
10. Don't vote on the 'helpfulness' of a review on your product or of someone else you are promoting as this won't be free from biases.

LEGAL WAYS TO GET AMAZON FBA REVIEWS

Incentivized reviews have dominated Amazon marketplace since the review feature cropped up. Most sellers on Amazon had become addicted to this incentivizing drug. Since Amazon banned incentivized reviews, most addicts are on hangovers while others are experiencing near-suicidal withdrawal symptoms.

You don't have to feel victimized. If you are a genuine seller with great product to sell, this is the moment to celebrate. Yes, it is like being a sprinter who relies on natural energy yet, you are denied a win by a competitor who is on steroids. Banning of steroids and enhancement substances will definitely be great news for you since you won't face unfair competition and your natural effort will be recognized and awarded.

To both the genuine competitors and the 'enhanced' competitors, there are many legal ways to get Amazon FBA reviews. The following are just but a few of them;

- Provide a superior quality product
- Provide excellent after-sale service
- Positively engage your customers

- Boost customer's overall product experience
- Build Goodwill
- Communicate regularly and effectively
- Update your customers on new product features and new product launches
- Offer extra benefit to customers that are not incentivizing
- Expose your product to greater viewership to increase potential customers

Key strategies to get Amazon FBA reviews in legal way

1. Marketing inserts
2. Email follow-up
3. Vine program
4. Leveraging traffic flow to increase probability of reviews

Marketing inserts

Marketing inserts are adverts placed inside the pack as part of the product.

Examples of marketing inserts include:

- Gift cards,
- Cross-sells,
- Thank you notes

The key aims of marketing inserts are:

- Build customer loyalty
- Boost revenues through cross-sales
- Personalized message delivery that can inspire positive reviews

Email follow-up

Email has remained the most effective form of written business communication over the internet. Modern email services have increased in terms of enhanced features that you can not only send an email in full colors but also graphics, videos and animated arts. This has boosted the richness of content.

One of the best ways of retaining customers is to keep communicating to them even after a sale has been made. This not only helps to reduce chances of negative reviews but also helps to improve chances of positive reviews.

Amazon Vine program

Amazon has created the only program in which you can get incentivized reviews. This is called Amazon Vine program. If you still feel that your customers need to be incentivized to make reviews, then, this is the only option available to you.

What is Amazon Vine

Amazon Vine is an invitation-only platform that encourages genuine and verified buyers to make independent and impartial review of targeted products in the Amazon marketplace.

What are the targeted products on Amazon Vine program?

Amazon Vine program targets new or pre-launched products.

How does Amazon Vine work?

Amazon sends periodic newsletter 'Vine Voices' notifying and informing Vine reviewers on the products enlisted in the Vine Program. Vine Reviewers are then invited or encouraged to apply to review products that they are interested in and are granted a go-ahead based on the qualification criteria.

Once an application is accepted, Amazon sends successful applicants sample products for them to review. After receiving the sample product (selected by Amazon itself, and not the seller), a reviewer is allowed up to 30 days to make an honest and unbiased review about the product.

After submitting the review, the review is allowed to retain the non-consumed part of it, (if possible) or return. The reviewer is not allowed to resale the unconsumed product.

How is Amazon Vine different from traditional review system?

The following are key differences between Amazon Vine system and traditional review system:

1. Amazon itself invites reviewers rather than you
2. There is no direct contact between the seller and the reviewer
3. There is no incentive for the reviewer to make biased review. This is because, unlike the seller, Amazon is a disinterested party that represents both the seller and the buyer.

Are Amazon Vine reviews incentivized?

Yes, Amazon Vine reviews are incentivized reviews. This is because reviewers are offered incentives by Amazon in form of Amazon Gift Cards as a form of reward for making their reviews. However, Amazon does not direct or encourage the reviewer to make positive review or make a certain kind of review rating. This is just like paying an independent auditor for audit, or paying an examiner for exams. You don't intend to influence the auditor or examiner but simply to pay them for service rendered or facilitate delivery of the service.

Thus, the key difference between Amazon's incentivized reviews and seller's incentivized reviews rests in the decisional independence accorded to the reviewer. Amazon grants the reviewer decisional independence which removes any element of biased direction. On the other hand, a seller would naturally like to influence the reviewer (or the reviewer might feel obliged) to make positive review and positive rating which is in itself biased and a deliberate misrepresentation of facts intended at deceiving potential buyer.

How does Amazon Vine benefit your FBA business?

Amazon Vine is the only incentivized way to get reviews for your products on Amazon. The following are ways by which you get to benefit from Amazon Vine as a vendor;

- You receive exposure by Vine Voices
- You receive genuine and reputable endorsement
- Your Goodwill grows
- Your gain more potential customers
- Your sales soars

What are Vine Voices?

Vine Voices refers to independent reviewers carefully selected by Amazon to review products on Amazon Vine program.

How are Amazon Vine Voices (reviewers) selected?

Amazon Vine Reviewers are selected through an invite-only program by Amazon. Though not explicitly mentioned by Amazon, the following are some of the criteria used to select Amazon Vine reviewers;

- Reputation – This refers to the quality of reviewing carried out by a potential Amazon Vine Reviewer. This quality is based on relevance, clarity, accuracy and helpfulness of the review to the intended audience – customers. It should be capable of improving their experience in making a buy decision. It should also be reliable in terms of helping customers make the right choice.
- Independence – The review should be unbiased and not hinged on incentivizing a customer to make a buy decision. It should be able to provided facts and information and let the customer make own judgment as to whether to buy or not.
- Expertise – The reviewer should have shown proven in-depth knowledge, understanding and skills in regard to a

particular niche within which the product under review falls.

- Experience- The reviewer should have a proven track record over reasonable time period for making reviews that meet that above mentioned criteria.

How can you enroll your products to Amazon Vine program?

Enrolling for Amazon Vine program requires you to first become Amazon Vendor. Before you choose to become Amazon Vendor, you must first understand the difference between being Amazon Seller and Amazon Vendor. Secondly, you must appreciate the pros and cons of the two options.

The following are the key differences between Amazon Seller and Amazon Vendor;

1. Amazon Seller operates via the Seller Central platform while Amazon Vendor operates via Vendor Central platform
2. Anyone can sell on Seller Central while only invitees can sell on Vendor Central.
3. Unlike Seller Central, you must have intellectual property ownership rights to be able to sell on Vendor Central.

Pros of Vendor Central

- Higher levels of consumer confidence – Amazon grants you "Sold by Amazon" seal of approval which boosts credibility of your products in the mind of the potential buyers. This makes your product more likely to be bought than similar products that lack this seal.
- Greater access to top-notch marketing tools – Amazon provides Vendor Central with more powerful marketing tools not available to Seller Central.
- A+ Content – This is content with highly enhanced features and attributes. This is extremely important for branding, product differentiation, advertising and Public Relations purpose. Vendor Central allows A+ Content while Seller Central does not.

Cons of Vendor Central

- Expensive analytics – Seller Central has high quality analytics for free. Vendor Central only offers simple, basic analytics. For you to get high quality analytics similar to those on Seller Central, you have to pay.
- Invite only – You must be invited by Amazon to become a member of the Vendor Central. Amazon allows you to 'request an Amazon buyer to send you an invitation'. However, this is not a guarantee. Nonetheless, there are

many vendors on Amazon, why not you? You too can become a Vendor.

- Less control – When you become a Vendor, Amazon becomes your retail. As such, you have no control over the price at which Amazon sells your products.

When should you consider becoming Amazon Vendor?

As we have seen above, Amazon Vendor has its pros and cons. To maximize on the pros so that they can profitably offset the cons, the following criteria should guide your choice to switch from Seller Central to Vendor Central:

- **Sales volume** – You should be capable of selling in high volumes. This way, even if Amazon shrinks your profit margin per item, you can still offset that by the huge overall profits gained from economies of scale offered by Amazon's huge global market.

- **Reputation** – If your product sales highly depend on reputation, then, consider becoming a Vendor. This way, you can beat competition.

Want to enjoy benefits of Vendor Central and Amazon Vine without invitation? Try Vendor Express!

Realizing the restrictions of Vendor Express, Amazon introduced Vendor Express as a hybrid alternative that allows those who own intellectual property rights; yet may not strictly meet the requirements of Vendor Central yet would like to supply their products to Amazon to enjoy some of the benefits of Vendor Central. Vendor Express targets those who can supply unique products and services such as artisans and those who do creative works. It is not very restrictive as anyone can join provided they have full ownership of intellectual property rights.

Vendor Express allows a vendor to enjoy some of the benefits of both Seller Central and Vendor Central.

FBA + Vendor Express: A great option?

Vendor Express allows two options:

- Fulfillment by Amazon (FBA)
- Fulfillment by Merchant (FBM) – This is whereby the vendor (merchant) fulfills customer Orders directly.

Thus, if you want to enjoy the benefits of FBA and yet enjoy the benefits of being a Vendor (of course without the suspense of waiting for an invitation), then, Vendor Express is the best deal for you.

What if I don't have intellectual property ownership? Try Private Label

Yes, you cannot become a vendor on Amazon if you don't have intellectual property rights to what you are supplying.

You don't have to sweat if you would like to be a vendor of a certain product and you don't have its intellectual ownership rights. You can still gain these rights via Private Labeling. A Private Label owner is deemed as an intellectual property owner in his/her own regard.

What is private labeling?

Private labeling refers to uniquely branding and differentiating an item so that it appears as originally coming from you. A significant number of items on the market today are private labels. Most items branded by celebrities are private labels. Examples of common items with private labels include sandals, apparels, mineral water, soft drinks, stationery, timepieces, cosmetics, and jewelry, among so many others.

Why private labeling?

Private labeling has become so popular these days, more so with the advent of Amazon FBA.

The following are key reasons as to why private labeling could be a good option for you:

- **Private labels are highly customized thus harder to benchmark by competitors** – Competitors like benchmarking themselves against competitors so that they can decide to undercut through pricing policy or publicity. However, since private labels are customized, they are unable to do so, unlike homogenous products.
- **Private label are relatively less costly to make** - Due to less overheads associated with high-end international brand, private labels are able to provide the same kind of quality product at a much cheaper price. Thus, more customers would be more willing to buy private labels
- **Private labels allow product differentiation** – Product differentiation is the best way to beat the competition, especially when you are dealing in homogenous products. Branding is paramount when it comes to marketing, and more so, in a global marketplace such as Amazon which has millions of products. Branding helps you create a unique image recognition in the minds of customers, create a separate marketing identity and boost customer loyalty as they attach their emotions to your brand.
- **Shorter chain of distribution** – With a private label, you can easily avoid middlemen by simply engaging the

producer, manufacturer, or dealer. This not only helps you to cut down on cost, but also time. If you are able to sell in higher quantities, then, you are more likely to receive quantity discounts and trade discounts which are extra benefits that add up to supernormal profits.

- **Niche specific customization** – Unlike major brands, private labels are easy to customize to meet the unique demands of a certain specific niche.

- **High levels of customer loyalty** – Due to niche-specific customizations, customer loyalty is high since they feel specially attached as their peculiar needs are catered for.

- **Unique value addition** – It is much easier to make a special formula of ingredients and branding just to enrich the experience of a peculiar market segment that is mostly ignored by large-scale general brands.

- **Control and autonomy** – With a private label, there is hardly any bureaucracy to hinder decision making. Thus, you are free to make quick independent decisions regarding your own private label.

- **Greater sense of ownership** – With a private label, you feel a greater sense of ownership since you can see the impact of your decisions regarding how you would like your private label to be. The name, logo, trademarks and others such features are all a result of your creative visualization.

- **Higher levels of customer satisfaction** – With private label, you have the flexibility to adjust to the peculiar needs of your customers as they express them. You can even have individualized items if the price affords.

Vendor Express: What you must not forget

Vendor Express is great. However, it is temporary and transitional. Amazon created Vendor Express as some sort of a vendor's incubator. It allows a not-so-well-established vendor to make baby-steps as the vendor matures.

Thus, before opting for Vendor Express, you must clearly understand the pros and cons of Vendor Central and make an informed decision.

How to get initial review organically

The toughest task is to get the initial reviews for your product. This is because you are most likely new to Amazon or even if you are experienced; your product is still new. This means that you will get customers who haven't found a review about your products and are more likely not to give one since a precedent has not been set. Thus, it must take special effort to inspire them to leave a review.

The following are some of the inspiring things you can do to attract customers to leave a review without incentivizing them:

- **Make a Great Listing** – A listing that has a professional touch will obviously stand out from the rest. Such a listing should have a proper title, great photo and good description. A photo is the first attraction yet leaves a lasting impression. It is important to invest in a professional photographer to come up with that impressive photo. The positive impression may trigger a customer to desire to leave a positive review.

- **Embrace good pricing strategy** – For a good pricing strategy, you have to understand your target market and its purchasing power. You also have to understand that your product is a new entrant and thus, you need to determine whether to use penetration pricing or skim pricing strategy. Penetration pricing is ideal if you are a new entrant yet there already exist stiff competition. Thus, you have to lower your price compared to competition, not really to make big profit but just to enter the market. Skim pricing is whereby you are a new entrant with a premium product that has virtually no competitors. Thus, you want to start with a higher price to skim the premium (which results into supernormal profits) and gradually lower your price as competition picks up. Skim pricing is ideal if you are dealing with a premium pricing where the target market has relatively high purchasing power.

- **Provide high quality products** – High product quality ensures that customers are satisfied. It is only satisfied customers that can volunteer to bother writing a great elaborate review about their experience with your product. Endeavor to have better quality than that being offered by your competitors. Even if the products are homogenous, trying to differentiation by altering and enhancing product features to make it unique. However, make sure that you don't overlook people's tastes and preferences. Justify customer expectations by promising what you can deliver. Be honest, otherwise customers may feel scammed and leave negative reviews which are even much worse than no review at all.

- **Carry out real-time inventory management** – Inventory management is one of the greatest challenges, especially if your portfolio is active and you are serving huge volumes. This too can happen when you are a new entrant such that you haven't mastered consumer demand patterns. When customers miss a product due to shortages, that's a missed opportunity for customer satisfaction and hence potential review. You also lose consumer loyalty and accompanying Goodwill. On the other hand, excess stock ties your capital, causes you to be surcharged for warehousing in increases the risk of expiry or obsolescence. There are four key criteria that you must establish to help you to properly manage inventory; Minimum stock level, Stock reorder level, Economic Order Quantity, Maximum Stock level. Minimum stock level is the level you can keep without running the risk of shortages. Stock re-order level is that level at which you must carry out stock replenishment, that is, order new stock. It is slightly higher than Minimum stock level. Economic Order Quantity refers to that quantity that you will order which in the most economical way bearing in mind quantity discounts, transportation cost, re-order cost, storage cost, insurance cost, among others. Maximum stock level is that level which if you stock beyond can result into higher storage costs and risks. Such storage costs and risks include spoilage, expire, obsolescence, insurance, pilferage, among others.

How to boost your potential for more reviews by increasing traffic

Just as in the conventional brick-and-mortar storefronts, being proximate to a location with huge traffic flow increases your chances of making more sales due to maximum exposure to a high number of potential customers.

The probability of receiving a review increases with the number of customers who buy your products. Thus, you must endeavor to increase traffic flow to your Amazon product page so that you increase probability of getting reviews.

There are two main sources of online traffic to your Amazon product page/listing;

- Amazon marketplace
- Outside Amazon marketplace

Driving traffic within Amazon marketplace into your listing

In order to successfully drive traffic already on Amazon marketplace into your listing, you need to employ the following strategies;

- **Optimize your listing for Amazon SEO** – SEO stands for Search Engine Optimization. People find products on Amazon based on search queries on Amazon search engine. To ensure that more customers arrive to your listing, then, your listing must use most commonly used search keywords. This way, most of the people who search for a product using the search keywords that you have incorporated in the text on your listing will be directed to your listing by the Amazon search engine. This is what we call SEO.

- **Choose appropriate fulfillment option** – As we have discussed before, there are two main types of fulfillment options; FBA (Fulfillment by Amazon) and FBM (Fulfillment by Merchant). Generally, based on Amazon search engine algorithm, FBA listings rank higher on the Search Engine Results Page (SERP) compared to FBM listings. Thus, it is to your advantage if you choose FBA as this will increase traffic flow to your listing, boost customer purchases and increase your probability of getting more reviews.

- **Focus on quality rather than quantity** – As much as higher traffic increases likelihood of you getting more reviews, this doesn't guarantee the quality of reviews. On Amazon, one quality positive review would be much better than 10 poor quality positive reviews. On the other hand, you would rather get no review at all than to get 10 negative reviews. To get high quality reviews, as we had discussed earlier, great customer experience is the key. Thus, high traffic will bring potential for reviews, but the quality of those reviews will depend on your customer experience.

Driving traffic from outside Amazon marketplace into your listing

It is great that Amazon marketplace has millions of visitors each day. However, a good number of them are already predetermined as to which shops they are visiting. While you can use strategies to convince them to visit your shop, you must not limit yourself to them. There are still billions out there!

The following are some of the common ways by which you can drive traffic from outside Amazon marketplace into your shop listing.

1. **Tap into social media traffic** – It is known that Facebook almost reaches 2 billion members. The entire social media space including Facebook, Twitter, Snapchat, Instagram, etc. collectively account for almost 4 Billion people. This is a huge source of traffic to tap into. You can have your product/niche page on Facebook and engage potential customers on it. You can use Twitter to broadcast breaking news about your new product launches, new

product features, among other things. You can use Instagram and Pinterest to show photos of latest enhancements. You can use your YouTube Channel to offer product use demonstrations. You can use StumbleUpon to spread information about your product discovery. You can do all these while directing traffic to your Amazon listing through linking.

2. **Make PPC advertisements** – Both Google and Facebook out of PPC. PPC is an acronym of Pay per Click. It is a 'democratic' form of voting where you the 'king' (customer) pay your servants (advertisers) only for work done (piece-work basis). PPC is the most popular form of advertisements. The quick rise of both Google and Facebook proves this. Yet, behind this multi-billion meteoric rise are multibillion empires from satisfied customers. You too also need to be a part of this multibillion dollar empire. To become part of them, simply create an advert (text, image, animation, video or a combination of some or all of these) as per the advertising platform requirements. Pay and upload the advert and let the advertising platform launch it to your target audience. Whenever potential customers click the advert, they are directed to your product listing.

3. **Use non-Amazon SEO** – We've already touched on Search Engine Optimization (SEO). As we have previously seen, Amazon has its own Search Engine. Thus, you can optimize you listing within Amazon. However, driving traffic from beyond Amazon will require you to device a different approach to SEO targeting popular search engines including Google, Bing, Yahoo, among others. This is mainly done through content marketing. You will need to create blogs, optimize them for SEO and redirect traffic flow from them to your own Amazon listing.

4. **Create a Niche Website** – To be successful in ecommerce, you need your very own online real estate. What you have on Amazon or social media networks is not your real estate but rentals. Your online real estate is your very own niche website. A niche website is a website specifically designed and developed to provide content and promote activities related to your niche products. This is a must-have if you intend to increase your passive income streams. Create a niche website and use links to redirect traffic to your Amazon listing. The great advantage of a niche website is that it is multifunctional. You can have a checkout on it linking to an Amazon store, you can have your own fully-fledged online shop and you too can have your own blog where to interact with your followers and customize and publish PR and other content.

5. **Publish Press Releases (PR) on regular or frequent basis** – When you have a following of readers and audience, they crave for your continued flow of information. Thus, you need to constantly feed them with latest information. There are several PR sites where you can launch your press release. Though reputable PR sites are difficult to list on (due to high standard of quality expected), once successful, you can get a huge volume of traffic to your site. However, with social media networks, you are not limited.

6. **Create product videos** – Videos provide means to receive communication from the two most powerful senses – sight and hearing. Thus, your communication to your potential customers is enchanced. Videos have become the most magnetic attraction of millennial generation. If your products are targeting millennials, then, creating "how-to" videos is the best way to attract them to your Amazon listing. Make a great "how-to" video about your product, upload on YouTube and simply link it to your Amazon listing.

7. **Subscribe to directory listing** – Online directories do the same task as the popular paper-based 'yellow pages' directories. Yet, unlike the paper-based 'yellow pages'

online directories provide more information, sophisticated presentations (including videos and animations), portability, global availability, etc. There are many directories offering niche placements and contact details. Providing these with links to your Amazon product page is the best way to utilize directory listing to drive traffic to your listing.

The proven practical legal tactics to get honest reviews

Just as we do have blackhat and whitehat tactics in SEO, we also have the same in reviews. Blackhat means illegal tactics that violate laid down policies. Whitehat tactics are those tactics that don't violate laid down policies.

The following of the legal tactics you can employ;

1. Network with Amazon's top-ranked reviewers

2. Engage prominent bloggers

3. Join Reviewers Groups on Facebook

4. Start your own club

5. Use Google Alerts and Social Mention

6. Make email requests for review

7. Create your own blog

8. Don't ignore unverified reviews

9. Participate in niche-specific forums

10. Respond to customer requests and opinions

11. Take advantage of survey tools

Network with with Amazon's top-ranked reviewers

Amazon has top-ranked reviewers. It is from some of these reviewers that Amazon taps its Amazon Voices.

The greatest challenge is to find these reviewers, especially if you are new to Amazon. Nonetheless, the following steps can help you;

(1) Visit product pages within your niche and check on reviewers

(2) Find out reviewers who have been indicated as "top reviewer" or those that have a high number of reviews

(3) Make a list of them as you visit various product pages

(4) Get their contacts by clicking on the links provided on their reviews so as to be led to their profile

(5) Contact about 5 of them, introduce your product and ask if they can make a honest, independent review of your product. They are knowledgeable in the field and would advice you how to go about in facilitating the process.

The advantage of top-ranked reviewer is that their reviews are given higher weight than those of ordinary reviewers.

Engage prominent bloggers

Each niche has prominent bloggers. However, the difficult task is to know or find them. To be able to find these blogers;

- Search for them in magazines relevant to your niche

- Search for them in a newspaper section where topics or articles related to your niche have been posted

- Use Google Search engine by typing in your niche and adding 'blog' or 'bloggers'. You can screen through the Search Engine Results Page for clues.

Once you have traced a prominent blogger, you can introduce yourself to him/her and introduce your product. You can then request to send a free sample for the blogger to review it on his/her blog.

When the blogger posts that product review on his/her blog many followers will be encouraged to try your product. It would be easy for the blogger to request them to leave an honest review of their experiences on your Amazon's product page.

This way, you will not have incentivized the blogger to make a review on your Amazon product's page. However, you will have succeeded in using the blogger to convince his/her followers, in non-incentivizing way, not only to try your product but also to post honest reviews on your Amazon's product page. Thus, the blogger will have helped you generate both sales and reviews.

Join Reviewers Groups on Facebook

Facebook has many reviewers groups within particular niches. You can join those groups and introduce your products and invite members to review your products. You can then invite those who make great reviews to do the same on your product's page on Amazon.

However, you should note that you are simply introducing and marketing your product into this group, not buying reviewers. You simply encourage those who have bought your product, experienced it and made their reviews in the group; to do the same on your Amazon page.

Start your own club

Should you not find the right Reviewers Group on Facebook, don't give up. You can create your own Reviewers club on the Facebook, specifically about your product niche. This will take longer to grow, but, it's your very own property. You have control over the discussion and you can have greater personal engagement with reviewers. Thus, it would be easier to convince them to leave a review on your Amazon product's page than you would convince those on Facebook already existing Group whom you will be competing with other sellers for the same request.

Use Google Alerts and Social Mention

When you have a brand that is getting popular, it is likely that your customers will be discussing it in other online forums which you are not aware of. Don't let that opportunity go. You can tap into it by using Google Alerts and Social Mention.

Simply create daily notifications on Google Alerts and Social Mention. These two popular tools will eavesdrop and sniff out any conversation involving your brand and notify you about it and where the conversation is.

Once you get to the conversation point, you can find creative ways to request the person making positive mentions about your brand/product to make a similar review on your Amazon product's page.

Make email request for review

One of the best ways to get customers to make review is through post-purchase follow-up. Email is one of the best ways to make post-purchase follow-up as it is not naggingly intrusive.

Prior to requesting for review, you need to be self-assured that you have done your best to satisfy the customer, based on your history of engagement. This way, the customer won't feel pressurized to make a review. A satisfied customer will be keen on further engagements and would be more willing to honour your request. Don't rush into making this request for review. At least, let it be the third email or later. Of course, the first post-purchase email will be about enquiring the customer experience with your product. The second email will be about responding to the feedback given and handling the issues raised. You could have a third one to offer some gift, coupon, or some other value addition such as extended warranty. Once you are assured that there are no further issues and the customer is satisfied, you can then request for the customer to make a review on your product's page.

In order to make an effective email request for review;

(1) Have a well laid out message

(2) Customize your message to that particular customer (avoid generic requests)

(3) Provide link to your product page with clear 'click' instruction

(4) Provide your instant contact detail e.g. phone number, skype, etc.

(5) Setup an instant alert on your phone so that you get alerted immediately the customer responds.

Create your own blog

Even the most prominent and famous bloggers were once beginners. Don't shy away from starting. You could feel that it is too late as you require quick reviews for your already launched product to soar up sales. Your effort won't be in waste. You could be surprised by how fast your blog could mature. It is not so much as to how long you have had the blog but how inspiring you are to your target audience.

Combining your powerful and inspiring message with strategies to drive traffic to your blog that we have so far discussed, including SEO, PPC, social media engagement and others, your blog could surprise you.

Steps:

(1) Start a blog for your product niche

(2) Regularly post SEO optimized articles on your blog about your products or niche with product images and links to your respective Amazon product pages.

(3) Share out your blog posts on social media

(4) Invite those who have bought your products to post on your blog. You are at liberty to incentivize them to post on your blog as this is not the same as leaving a review on your Amazon product's page.

(5) You can request your followers, each individually, via email or other means, who have bought your products and posted their experience to make honest review on Amazon

Don't ignore unverified reviews

Under latest Amazon review policy, it has classified reviews into two categories;

- Verified reviews

- Unverified reviews

Verified reviews are those reviews;

- Made by a verified purchaser

- A purchaser who as bought an item at a price that is at least 50% of the ordinary price

- A purchaser who has made purchases on Amazon accumulating to at least $50 and above

- They are marked by Amazon as 'verified review'

Unverified reviews

- Made by someone who has not bought your product from Amazon but other places e.g. eBay, Shopify, Walmatt and even off-line stores.

Why unverified reviews are different from verified reviews;

- They are not considered for Amazon's Best Seller Rank (BSR)

- They don't contribute traffic metrix on Amazon

- They are marked by Amazon as 'unverified review'

Why are they still important?

Unverified reviews, if positive, will still contribute towards endorsing your product and thus help the customer make informed decision. Though they will not be considered with the same reliability as verified reviews, but, they are better than nothing.

Participate in niche-specific forums

There are many forums that are niche-specific. Find those that are relevant to your niche. Frequently participate in them as you introduce your products. Once you have become familiar, it would be easy for those customers you have engaged with on those forums to give opinions about your products. If the opinions are positive, this will encourage more potential customers to try out your product. You can then approach those who have positive opinion about your product to make review on your Amazon product page.

Respond to customer requests and opinions

One of the leading causes of negative reviews or lack of reviews at all is not improving customer experience of your product by not responding to customer's needs.

To avoid this, be frequent on your product's page under the comments/forum section and respond to customer inquiries, opinions and even complaints. Don't shy away from an unsatisfied customer. That could be your most loyal customer if you convert him/her.

By responding to requests, inquiries, opinions and complains, you boost your engagement level with your customers. Other customers who had the same issues will feel appropriately addressed. Potential customers too will feel confident that you will be able to address their issues appropriately once they buy your product.

You can take advantage of those responses by requesting those satisfied customers to leave a honest review.

Take advantage of survey tools

Sometimes you would like to increase the chances of getting posive reviews without specifically asking the customer to make positive review as this will flout Amazon policy. This is so important when your product is still new to the market, though you can still use survey tool at any other stage.

The advantage of survey tools is that, you will be able to gauge what you are likely going to get from a particular customer in terms of rating. Yet, the survey will make the customer feel that this is an unbiased professional undertaking requiring him/her to make an independent assessment.

To achieve this:

(1) Design a survey questionnaire inquiring about 4 to 5 key areas of your product or customer satisfaction.

(2) Let the customer respond by rating each key area from 1 star to 5 stars

(3) Set an 'invitation to review' page to appear after the interview for those customers who have had a rating of 3.5 and above. It should have 'click button' which they will clink and get linked to the product's page to leave a review.

(4) Set a "Thank you page" as the final page to those who have rated below 3.5

Popular survey tools that you can easily customize include

- Google Forms

- SurveyMonkey

- Typeform

- Survey Plant

- Survey Gizmo

- Zoho Survey

You can send link links to the survey tool via email. If possible, call the customer to notify him/her of the survey. This will increase the probability of the customer actually taking the survey.

CONCLUSION

Thank you for acquiring and reading this book.

This book is the best guide on how to make legit reviews to avoid being banned by Amazon, leverage your reviews to push-up sales and earn supernormal profits.

I hope you have been able to acquire relevant information regarding latest changes in Amazon FBA Review system, mistakes to avoid while getting reviews and legal ways to get Amazon FBA reviews. It is also my sincere hope that you have been able to share with others information on how to acquire this book so that they too can have a reference source from which they can continue benefiting from its information.

Good luck!

www.ingramcontent.com/pod-product-compliance
Lightning Source LLC
Chambersburg PA
CBHW071504210326
41597CB00018B/2687